Easter

LABURNUM
PRESS

Katie Dicker

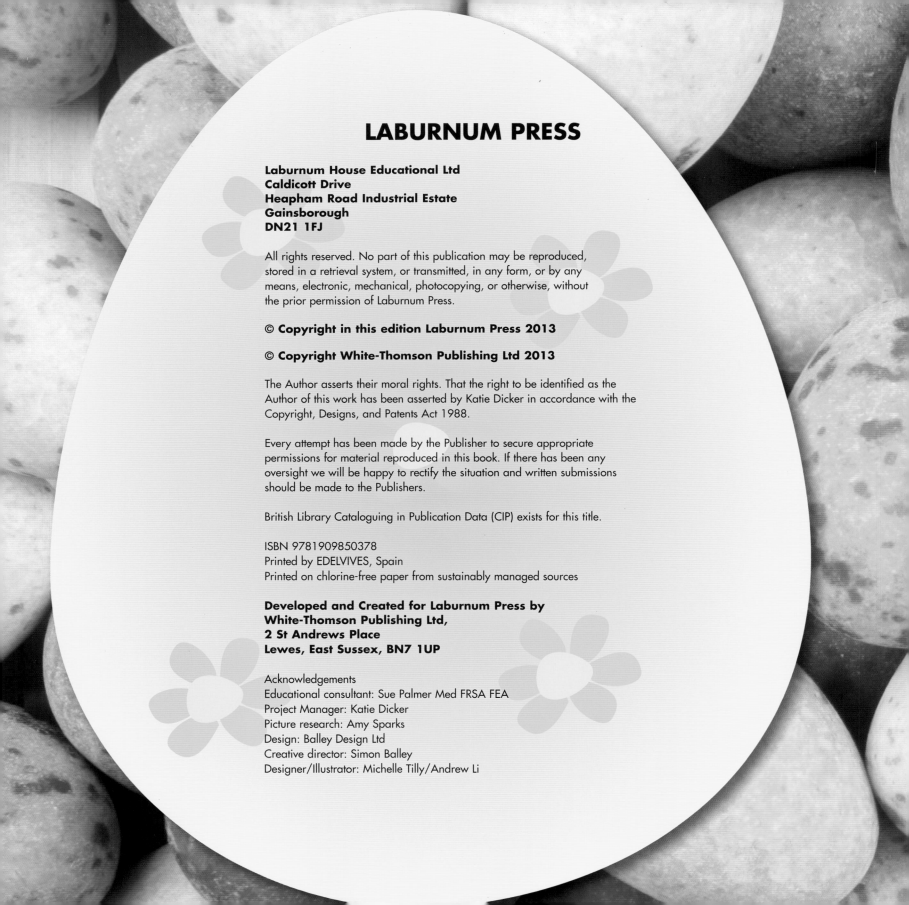

LABURNUM PRESS

Laburnum House Educational Ltd
Caldicott Drive
Heapham Road Industrial Estate
Gainsborough
DN21 1FJ

British Library Cataloguing in Publication Data (CIP) exists for this title.

ISBN 9781909850378
Printed by EDELVIVES, Spain
Printed on chlorine-free paper from sustainably managed sources

Developed and Created for Laburnum Press by
White-Thomson Publishing Ltd,
2 St Andrews Place
Lewes, East Sussex, BN7 1UP

Acknowledgements
Educational consultant: Sue Palmer Med FRSA FEA
Project Manager: Katie Dicker
Picture research: Amy Sparks
Design: Balley Design Ltd
Creative director: Simon Balley
Designer/Illustrator: Michelle Tilly/Andrew Li

Contents

You can see sheep and their lambs in the fields.

Back to life

I think of Jesus when I pray.

Long ago, a man called Jesus died on the cross.

6

bright

He came back to life after three days.

At Easter, we celebrate this miracle.

7

The Easter story

The Easter story is told in a book called the Bible.

New beginnings

Chirp!

The Easter story is also

a celebration of new life.

It reminds us that every day can be a new beginning for us all.

sunrise

Family and friends

Watch out!

At Easter, we spend time with members of our family...

12

... and invite our friends round for dinner.

13

Time to Celebrate

Tra-la-la!

These children are wearing their Easter costumes.

14

chick

What would YOU use to decorate an Easter bonnet?

15

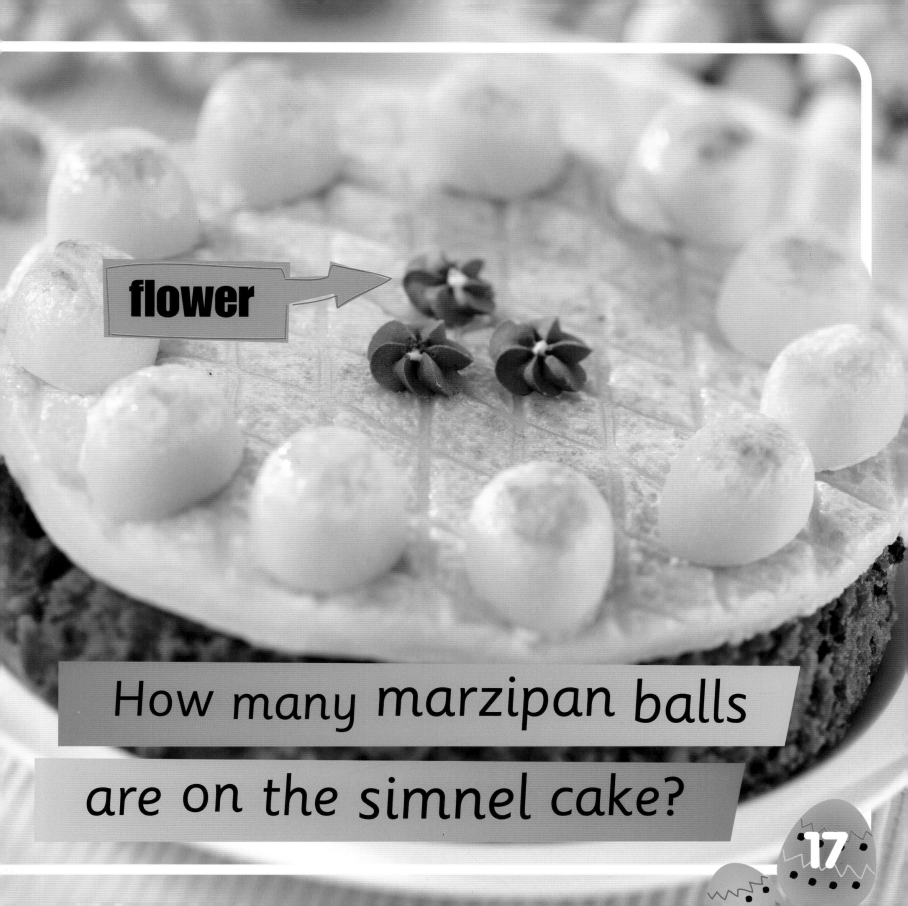

flower

How many marzipan balls
are on the simnel cake?

17

spots

What Easter egg patterns do YOU like to paint?

19

Easter worldwide

blossom

In Germany, people hang Easter eggs from the trees.

Look at our flowers!

These boys in Central America are part of an Easter parade.

Notes for adults

Sparklers books are designed to support and extend the learning of young children. The **Food We Eat** titles won a Practical Pre-School Silver Award, the **Body Moves** titles won a Practical Pre-School Gold Award and the **Out and About** titles won the 2009 Practical Pre-School Gold Overall Winner Award. The books' high-interest subjects link in to the Early Years curriculum and beyond. Find out more about Early Years and reading with children from the National Literacy Trust (www.literacytrust.org.uk).

Themed titles
Easter is one of four **Celebrations** titles that encourage children to learn about annual festivals and different cultures around the world. The other titles are:

Christmas   **Divali**   **Chinese New Year**

Areas of learning
Each **Celebrations** title helps to support the following Early Years Foundation Stage areas of learning:
Personal, Social and Emotional Development
Communication, Language and Literacy
Problem Solving, Reasoning and Numeracy
Knowledge and Understanding of the World
Physical Development
Creative Development

Making the most of reading time
When reading with younger children, take time to explore the pictures together. Ask children to find, identify, count or describe different objects. Point out colours and textures. Allow quiet spaces in your reading so that children can ask questions or repeat your words. Try pausing mid-sentence so that children can predict the next word. This sort of participation develops early reading skills.

Follow the words with your finger as you read. The main text is in Infant Sassoon, a clear, friendly font designed for children learning to read and write. The labels and sound effects add fun and give the opportunity to distinguish between levels of communication. Where appropriate, labels, sound effects or main text may be presented phonically. Encourage children to imitate the sounds.

As you read the book, you can also take the opportunity to talk about the book itself with appropriate vocabulary such as "page", "cover", "back", "front", "photograph", "label" and "page number".

You can also extend children's learning by using the books as a springboard for discussion and further activities. There are a few suggestions on the facing page. The Internet also has many teaching resources about annual festivals. For example, see www.365celebration.com and www.underfives.co.uk.

Pages 4–5: Spring in the air

Help children to make a collage illustrating new life in spring. Use card, tissue paper and textured fabrics to show flowers growing, chicks hatching and baby animals in the fields. Talk to children about the four seasons and how they differ. What festivals are linked to particular seasons?

Pages 6–7: Back to life

Explain to children that Easter is a Christian celebration and talk to them about the resurrection of Jesus. Help to hone children's understanding with some activities, such as making and decorating a cross. Try making an Easter garden, with a stone that rolls away. You could sow grass seeds in the miniature garden, for children to cut the grass with safety scissors as it grows.

Pages 8–9: The Easter story

Encourage children to put on an Easter play to explain the Easter story to others. Children may also enjoy making and writing their own Easter cards, illustrating part of the Easter story. Ask children to talk about who they would like to give a card to, and why.

Pages 10–11: New beginnings

Talk to children about different life cycles in nature and how each day, week and year can be a new beginning for us all. Help children to make a chick from a yellow feather duster or a yellow wool pom-pom ball. You could stick felt on for the eyes and beak and use pipe cleaner legs.

Pages 12–13: Family and friends

Children may enjoy preparing a table for a special meal with family or friends. Help children to make and write some invitations and place names. Encourage the children to count as they lay the table for dinner. Are there enough knives and forks to go round? Can the children make a table decoration with spring flowers?

Pages 14–15: Time to celebrate

Help children to learn some Easter songs, such as "Hot Cross Buns" or "Easter parade". Encourage the children to make their own Easter bonnet. You could use a paper plate attached with ribbons and decorated with tissue paper or fresh flowers. Boys may prefer to make an Easter crown (see http://www.enchantedlearning.com/crafts/hats/flowerhat, for example).

Pages 16–17: Special food

Help children to make some Easter biscuits or chocolate nests filled with mini eggs. You could also make some model hot cross buns from clay or a model card simnel cake, filled with mini eggs inside. Talk to children about the symbolism of the cake. The marzipan balls represent Jesus' disciples. There should be 12, but one is missing because Judas had betrayed Jesus.

Pages 18–19: Easter eggs

Organise an Easter egg hunt. Who can find the most eggs? Where were they hidden? Encourage the children to decorate their own hard-boiled eggs with bright colours and patterns. Talk to children about the tradition of surprise gifts and the Easter bunny. Children may also enjoy making a bunny mask or trying to hop like a rabbit.

Pages 20–21: Easter worldwide

Explain to children that Easter is celebrated around the world, but not by everyone. Encourage children to talk about how their family celebrate Easter (or another festival). Make a collage to illustrate different Easter traditions around the world. Use the Internet to help you. Some examples include special flower decorations in Spain and Mexico, painting eggs red in Greece, and an autumn celebration in Australia.

Index

Picture acknowledgements:
Alamy: 14 (Liba Taylor); **Corbis:** cover girl (Heide Benser), 7 (Mike Kemp/ Rubberball), 15 (Bo Zaunders), 18 (Jutta Klee), 20 (Mark Bolton); **Dreamstime:** cover hedge (Gualberto Becerra), cover birds (Piotr Sikora), cover tree (confidential info), 2-3 mini eggs (Richard Griffin), 4 (confidential info), 9 (Ron Chapple Studios), 13 (Anthony Harris), 22-23 mini eggs (Richard Griffin), 24 mini eggs (Richard Griffin); **Getty Images:** 11 (Jakob Helbig), 12 (Image Source), 16 (Getty Images); **Photolibrary:** 6 (Stockdisc), 8 (Jose Luis Pelaez Inc), 17 (Foodfolio Foodfolio), 19 (Corbis), 21 (Robin Lubbock); **Shutterstock:** cover field (Majeczka), 5 (Eric Gevaert), 10 chick (snowhite), 10 hay (Gualberto Becerra).